The Animalympics' Guide to The Olympics

by Margery Steinberg

A Tempo Star Book

Distributed by Ace Books
Grosset & Dunlap, Inc., Publishers
New York, N.Y. 10010
A Filmways Company

Contents

What Are the Olympics?

Often called the world's greatest sporting event, the Olympic Games are held every four years at different sites. The participants are a large cast of amateur athletes from various countries, and the events are both sporting and festive.

Various sports organizations of each participating country hold their own competitions to send the best athletes to the Olympics. Eligibility requirements for all contestants are: citizenship in the country he or she represents; and amateur status in his or her sport. (Amateur means never having competed for money.) All expenses of the competition are paid by voluntary contributions to Olympic funds and subsidies of participating national governments.

Although participants represent their countries, the emphasis is on the achievement of the individual athlete. No country receives any official Olympic recognition as being "the winner." Many great medal-winning athletes have achieved worldwide fame for thier record-breaking Olympic performances.

The number and kind of sports vary from year to year. The International Olympic Committee has designated specific summer sports and winter sports that can be included in the program. Separate competitions for women are conducted in selected sports. Women athletes are also permitted to compete with men in some sports.

Origin of the Olympic Games

Olympia, the home of the ancient Olympic Games, is said to have been established by Hercules himself. Olympian gods were said to have been the first competitors there.

The Olympic Games were the greatest festival of the mighty Greek nation. Beginning in 776 B.C., the games were held every four years, and included religious, athletic, and cultural events. The athletic contests were highly organized and run under strict rules. Participants believed that they were honoring the Greek gods. Winners of the games were recognized by all the Greeks. No gifts or rewards were given, but the symbol of honor, the olive wreath, was placed on the head of each victor.

The ancient Olympic Games took place every four years for some 1200 years. They survived many political and social changes, but in the year A.D. 393, the Emperor Theodosius forbade the Games.

Not celebrated again until 1896, the games were revived by Baron Pierre de

Coubertin. The first modern games took place in Athens, the closest practical site to the ancient Olympia. Many of the old Olympic contests were used, and some new games were added. Thirteen nations, including America, sent a total of 285 men to compete in the first modern games. Competition was in ten different sports and forty-two gold medals were awarded to the winners.

Because of the success of the first modern Olympics, the games were officially celebrated in different countries every fourth year, except for interruptions caused by world wars.

The Olympic Creed

"The most important thing in the Olympic Games is not to win but to take part. The essential thing in life is not to conquer but to fight well."

These words are part of a speech given by the Baron Pierre de Coubertin of France in 1894. It is because of his efforts that the modern-day Olympics were founded.

Following the Franco-Prussian War of 1870, de Coubertin was interested in helping soldiers who had been defeated in the war. He thought that he could bring honor back to these young men by restaging the glorious athletic and cultural events of ancient Greece. His aim in reviving the Olympic Games was to build the character of young people through participation in competitive sports. He also hoped to promote peace and goodwill among nations.

The Olympic Creed

The five rings of the pawprint is the Animalympics flag and symbol of world peace.

The Olympic Flag

Flying high over the Olympic Stadium is the symbolic Olympic flag. It made its first appearance at the Antwerp Games in 1920.

The flag's five interlocked rings of blue, yellow, black, green, and red represent the athletic union of earth's five continents (Europe, Asia, Africa, Australia, and the Americas). The spirit of fair competition and brotherhood are represented by this symbol. The colors were chosen because at least one of them appears in the flag of every nation of the world.

The Olympic motto appears underneath the rings on the flag. It is written in Latin, and its words *Citius, Altius, Fortius* are understood internationally to mean *swifter, higher, stronger*. Competitive Olympic athletes indeed try to run faster, jump higher, and throw more strongly.

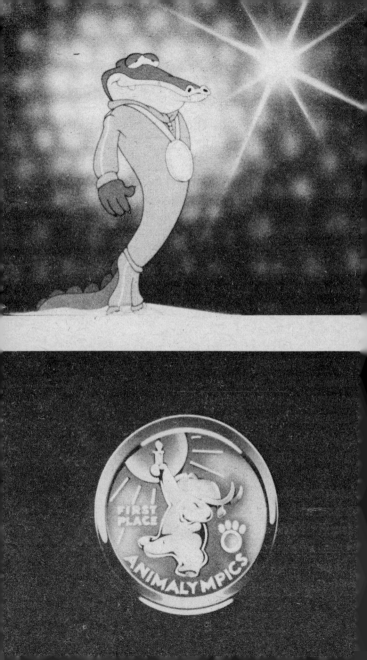

Olympic Medals

The competitive spirit is high among Olympic participants. Each one is striving to do his or her best, and to win a coveted Olympic medal.

The prize medals and diplomas are designed and manufactured by the Olympic Games Organizing Committee of the host city. First prize is a gold medal, which is actually a silver medal that is gilded with at least 6 grams of fine gold, and a diploma. Second prize is a silver medal and a diploma. Third prize is a bronze medal and a diploma. Fourth, fifth, and sixth place contestants are awarded diplomas. In the case of a tie, duplicate awards are presented.

A brief ceremony follows each event. The president of the International Olympic Committee, or his designated representative, presents the awards to first, second, and third place winners. As each of the national anthems is played, the national flags of the three winners are hoisted on flagpoles in positions of honor.

Opening Ceremony

The parade of athletes is one of the most thrilling ceremonies of the Games. The athletes, many dressed in their native costumes, march into the stadium. The Greeks, founders of the Olympic Games, always lead the parade. The other nations follow in alphabetical order, except for the host nation, which marches last. Each country selects its own standard-bearer to display its national flag.

The chief of state of the host nation is invited to salute the opening ceremony. The president of the International Olympic Committee opens by saying, "I have the honor to invite (chief of state) to proclaim open the Games of the (twenty-first, etc.) Olympiad of the modern era, initiated by Baron Pierre de Coubertin in 1896." The chief of state responds, "I declare open the Games of (year) celebrating the (twenty-first; etc.) Olympiad of the modern era."

The band then plays the Olympic Hymn, composed in 1896 by Spiron Samara with words by Costis Palamas of Greece. The Olympic flag is raised, and another flag is presented to the mayor of the host city to fly at the City Hall for the next four years.

The Olympic torch is brought to the stadium by a single runner or by a team of runners. The flame is symbolic of the Olympic torch that was originally lit by rays from the sun at ancient Olympia. The flame will burn continuously for the duration of the Games.

Hundreds of peace doves are released into the stadium, bringing the formal ceremony to a close and signaling that the Games are ready to begin.

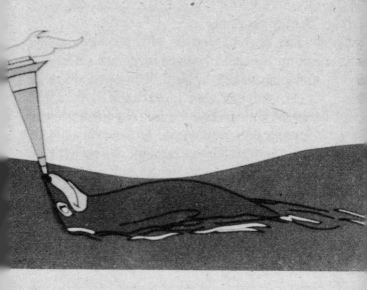

Closing Ceremony

The athletes are not separated by nationality in this emotion-filled parade. They display their bonds of Olympic friendship and fellowship. Waving their hats, jackets, and scarves toward the audience, the athletes express their gratitude. Words of thanks are given to the host city, and the International Olympic Committee President says, "I call upon the youth of all countries to assemble four years from now at _____, there to celebrate with us the Games of the _____ Olympiad (or the _____ Olympic Winter Games)."

The flags of Greece, of the host country, and of the next host country are all raised and beautifully lighted. The band plays as the Olympic flame is extinguished. Then the Olympic Hymn is played and the Olympic flag is lowered and carried out of the stadium. The ceremony closes with an impressive five-gun salute.

The Winter Games

Skiing and Ice Skating were included in some of the early modern Olympic Games as demonstration sports. But it wasn't until 1924 that the Winter Games became a formal Olympic program. In the Charmonix, France, Games of 1924, some 293 athletes represented sixteen nations in sixteen events. The 1976 Games in Insbruck, Austria, had 1261 participants from thirty-seven nations and thirty-seven events. For the 1980 Olympics, thirty-eight events have been scheduled.

Winter Olympic sports include events in skiing, sledding, skating, and tobogganing. One interesting concern of Winter Games host cities is that they must be prepared for the failure of Mother Nature. Ski slopes and sledding runs are equipped with artificial snow-making devices—just in case it doesn't snow.

Lake Placid, 1980

Many people were puzzled by the selection of Lake Placid, New York, to host the 1980 Winter Games. They wondered how such a small, isolated village could handle an event as big as the Olympics.

Actually, the town is quite excited about the event and is working hard to prepare for it. Lake Placid's main source of income is tourism, which has a short three-month season. During the rest of the year only some 3000 people live there. The Olympic Games will surely bring in many more tourists, who will spend a considerable amount of money in the town.

Lake Placid hosted the Winter Olympics in 1932 and some of the buildings used then are still standing. In addition, all of the new construction costs are being financed by federal and state governments.

The main problem facing the organizers is housing for spectators. Many will have to scatter throughout surrounding towns to find rooms—some as far as two and a half hours away. Plans are being made to complete railroad service throughout the area in time for the Olympics.

The 1984 Winter Olympics are scheduled to be held in Sarajevo, Yugoslavia.

Biathlon

Biathlon is a race that involves cross-country skiing and target shooting. There are individual races as well as team relays.

The course is 20 kilometers long, or about 12 miles. Contestants carry special non-automatic rifles. Stopping at four firing stations, they shoot five rounds each at four different targets. A penalty of two minutes is added to a participant's score for each target missed. The object of the race is to finish the course in the fastest time.

This event was included in Olympic competition before 1936. Because the skills used were considered more military than sporting, the biathlon was dropped after that year. It was reintroduced in the Winter Games of 1960, and has been included in every Olympiad since then.

Bobsledding

Bobsledding got its name because the riders would "bob" to increase the speed of the sled. The brakeman gives the command and the men lean forward after leaning backward as far as possible. When the whole team works together these movements do increase their racing speed.

But the sport is also a dangerous one. The sled, once it gets moving, travels at speeds of up to 89 miles per hour. Mounted on high runners, the bobsled can easily tip over, spilling the team all over the course.

Two contests are included in the Olympics—the two-man Bob and the four-man Bob.

Luge

A Luge is a small sled.

Originally child's play, sledding has become a highly competitive sport. The sled used in the Olympics is a vehicle of speed and risk.

The luge has no braking or steering mechanism. Racers lie flat on their backs on the sled. By changing their body positions they control and steer the luge.

The events are held on a specially built, cavelike ice track on which the luge travels making 360° loops and turns. Zooming some 1200 meters down the mountainside, it reaches speeds of 90 miles per hour. So, much athletic skill is needed to make a successful run.

Single and two-man events are held for men. Women compete in only single seater contests. A race consists of four runs by each participant or team.

The lowest total time wins.

Ice Hockey

Ice Hockey is played by six-man ice skating teams consisting of a goalie, a center, two forwards (wings), and two quarters. The game is played on a rink that, in Olympic competition, measures 200 feet long by 100 feet wide. Goal nets are located at either end of the rink.

The object of the game is to score goals. Using a hockey stick, players move a puck (a flat circular rubber disk) around the rink. The team that has the puck charges for the other team's goal net. The defending team tries to keep the puck out of their goal. The goalie, wearing padded clothing and a face mask, protects his team's goal.

Play begins with a "face-off." One member of each team stands in the center circle and tries to get control of the puck.

If a player breaks a rule, he is given a penalty and must leave the game for a period of time. Some fouls for which penalties are given are high-sticking (raising the hockey stick above the shoulders), kneeing, elbowing, spearing, tripping, hooking, clipping, and fighting. Different penalty times from two minutes to ten minutes, or even total removal from the game, depend on the seriousness of the foul.

Olympic competition is run on a tournament basis. Points are awarded for wins (2 points), ties (1 point), and losses (0 points). The team with the most points wins.

Canadian teams won most of the ice hockey events until 1960. Since that time many Canadians have been unable to participate in Olympic competition because they are already professional ice hockey players. The U.S.S.R. has recently been producing many of the winning teams in this sport.

Figure Skating

The Figure Skating events are among the most popular of today's Olympic winter sports. Competition is in Men's, Women's, Pairs, and most recently, Ice Dancing.

The Olympic figure skater must follow a rigid progression of movements from the very simple to the most difficult. These "compulsory figures" are graded by the judges and account for sixty percent of a contestant's total score. Jumps, circles, turns, and spins are included in each program.

The rest of the skater's score (40 percent) is based on "free skating." A skating program set to music is performed by each contestant. Consideration is given to the technical development and the artistic presentation of the routine.

Pairs consist of one man and one woman who perform a short program of compulsory figures and a free skating program. Both marks are added to determine the final score.

In Ice Dancing, the two competitors must perform the same steps or figures. The team's program consists of compulsory figures and free skating. Originality and interpretation are considered in the scores.

Speed Skating

Speed Skating has not gained much worldwide acceptance even though it is in the Olympics. Few countries other than the United States, Canada, Russia, and the Scandinavian countries have shown interest in this sport.

An oval ice track is the setting for speed skating competition. Two skaters race against each other in separate lanes of the

track. Because the inside lane is shorter than the outside lane, the skaters change lanes at a crossover point after each lap. (One time around the track.) This is to insure that each skater goes exactly the same distance.

Men compete in 500-meter, 1000-meter, 1500-meter, 5000-meter, and 10,000-meter races. The women's contests are the 500-meter, 1000-meter, 1500-meter, and 3000-meter distances.

The skater in each race scoring the fastest time wins.

Skiing

No one is sure whether the ski or the snowshoe came first. However, both were used as a means of travel in snow-covered countries long ago. Skiing has been practiced as a sport for only about one century. It is one of the most popular winter pastimes for Americans.

Skiing was a demonstration sport in some of the earlier modern Olympic Games. In 1924, when winter sports gained formal recognition, skiing became part of the Olympic program.

Competitive skiing is in two categories—Alpine events and Nordic events. The different contests require different skills and provide some of the greatest winter thrills.

Nordic Skiing

Participants call Nordic Skiing a lonely but beautiful sport. They feel so good being out in the woods among the wonders of nature and the cold white snow.

Cross-Country Skiing is one of the Nordic events. There are both sprint (short distance) and marathon (long distance) races. Courses include both uphill and downhill runs, as well as some flat sections. The skis themselves only have toe bindings. Racers move with a running-like action, using their heels to help them pick up speed.

Relay teams as well as individual men and women compete to achieve the fastest times. The men's events are: the 15-kilometer (9.3-mile), 30-kilometer (18.6-mile), and 50-kilometer (31-mile) races; and the four-man, 10-kilometer (6-mile) relay race. The women's events are: the 5-kilometer (3-mile) and 10-kilometer (6.2-mile) races; and the three-woman, 5-kilometer (3-mile) relay race.

Soviet and Scandinavian participants have won many of these events over the years.

Good judgment is needed by participants in cross-country skiing. As weather condi-

tions and snow conditions change during the races, skiers must apply different types of waxes to their skis. If the wrong wax is used, they may be slowed down or in danger of being hurt.

Ski Jumpers fly through the air with grace and good posture. The skill of their takeoff and landing are included in the competitor's scores. Jumpers require the speed of downhill with the ability of an acrobat to be successful in ski jump events.

In the Olympics there are two ski jumping events for men only—one from a 90-meter hill and the other from a 70-meter hill. Each participant performs two jumps and is marked on distance and style. The highest and lowest points are dropped and the other scores are added together.

If a jumper fails, he loses points but is not disqualified. The highest scorer wins.

One final contest in this sport is the Nordic combined event. It consists of three ski jumps from 70-meter hills and cross-country skiing on a 15-kilometer course. A total score determines the winner.

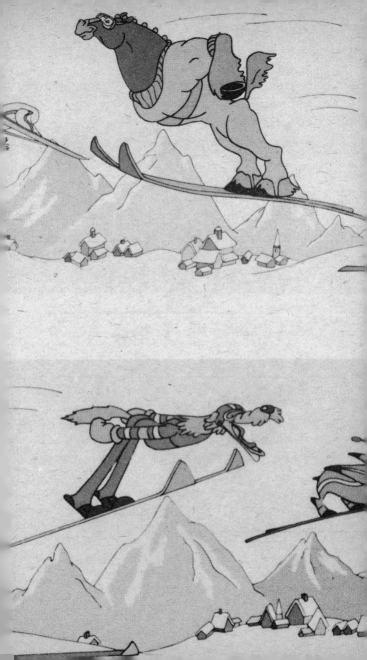

Alpine Skiing

Watching the Slalom event you are likely to see a skier whizzing downhill at 70 miles per hour and turning through flag "gates" that mark the course. Competitors ski along this run in the fastest time they can while skillfully passing with both feet between the sets of flags. Skiers are disqualified if they miss any of the gates.

The Downhill event is a high-speed race against the clock. Each participant skis down the predetermined course and has his or her time recorded. Gates mark the run to prevent skiers from taking unnecessary risks. The person scoring the lowest time wins.

The Giant Slalom contest combines the speed of downhill racing with the skill of the slalom. There are at least thirty gates in this event and they are much farther apart than in the slalom. The course is much longer than in any other Alpine race. Men complete two runs and receive a total score. Women ski only one run.

Jean-Claude Killy, a world-champion skier, is famous for winning gold medals in all three Alpine events in the 1968 Games at Grenoble, France.

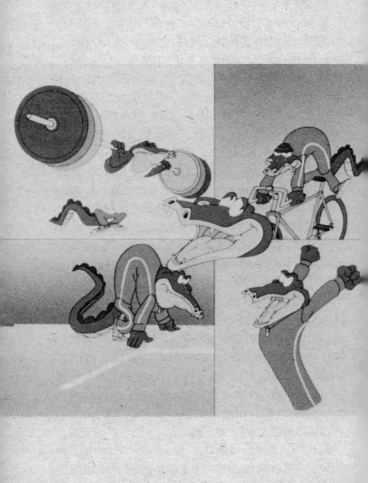

The Summer Games

The contests that were included in the first modern Olympics in 1896 are now referred to as the "Summer Games." There are twenty-one recognized men's sports and eleven women's sports in this series, including the very popular Track and Field events; the team sports of Basketball, Field Hockey, Soccer, and Volleyball; the Swimming and Diving competitions; and various other land and water sports.

Participation in the Olympics has grown considerably since the Athens Games of 1896. Only ten nations participated in a total of forty-two events that year, as compared to 88 nations and 199 events in the 1976 Montreal Games.

Moscow, 1980

The International Olympic Committee chooses the city in which a future Olympiad's Games will take place at least six years in advance. Therefore, in 1974 the site of the 1980 Summer Games was selected. Moscow, U.S.S.R., will be the host city and competition will take place from July 19 to August 3. A total of 200 events are planned.

Plans are already being made for the 1984 Games. The committee voted the site to be Los Angeles, California.

Wrestling

The most powerful men in the world exhibit their strength and skill in these Olympic contests. Wrestling as a sport dates back to the ancient Olympic Games. In prehistoric times, man learned wrestling as a skill in his struggle for survival.

Two types of wrestling are used in Olympic competition. In Greco-Roman style, the wrestler tries to make his opponent touch the ground with any part of his body except the feet. Neck and head holds are not permitted. In Free-style (also known as catch-as-catch-can) competitors may use holds on all parts of the body.

Olympic wrestling is divided into ten weight classes for each style: Light Flyweight (maximum 105¾ pounds), Flyweight (114½ pounds), Bantamweight (125¾ pounds), Featherweight (138¾ pounds), Lightweight (149¾ pounds), Welterweight (163 pounds), Middleweight (180¾ pounds), Light-Heavyweight (198¼ pounds), Heavyweight (202¼ pounds), and Super-Heavyweight (220¼ pounds).

During each bout contestants are awarded points for different moves. Each score is converted into penalty points. The winner of the competition is the wrestler with the least number of penalty points.

Swimming

The Olympic Games are responsible for advancing the popularity of Swimming as a competitive sport. Since its introduction in the 1896 Athens Games, Swimming has played an important role in the Olympics.

In 1912 at Stockholm, Sweden, America produced its first great swimmer. Duke Kahanamoku of Hawaii introduced the "flutter kick" to increase a swimmer's speed. He then became the first man to swim 100 yards in less than a minute—fifty-three seconds, to be exact!

The great Johnny Weissmuller broke Duke's record in 1924 at Paris. He set world records in the 100-meter and 400-meter freestyle events. In 1950 he was named "the greatest swimmer of the past 50 years." This surprised many people, for they knew Johnny as the star of many *Tarzan* movies, but had no idea he was such an outstanding swimmer.

Another champion Olympic swimmer later played the movie role of Tarzan. In 1932 at Los Angeles, American Clarence (Buster) Crabbe won the 400-meter free-style competition.

Mark Spitz is the most recent American

swimming champion. He won seven gold medals, all in record-breaking times.

Olympic swimmers compete in events using four strokes—Freestyle, Backstroke, Breaststroke, and Butterfly Stroke. Olympic pools are 50 meters in length and are divided into eight equal lanes. Each event is run in the following order: heats, semifinals, and a final. The winner is the swimmer scoring the fastest time. Men and women compete as individuals and as teams in this event.

The Diving competitions are scored on the basis of points from 0 to 10. Judges consider the degree of difficulty of the dive and how well the dive is performed.

Platform Diving takes place on a diving board that is 30 feet, 5 inches above the water. Divers perform required and voluntary dives for which they are scored. The highest and lowest marks are discounted in determining the final results. The men and women having the highest total are the winners.

Springboard Diving is scored in the same way as platform diving. Participants perform from a springboard that is 9 feet, 10 inches above the water.

Water Polo is a team game played in a

swimming pool with a ball. The number of goals scored by each team in a match earns them points. The team totaling the greatest number of match points wins the title. The Hungarians have won the most victories in this Olympic sport since 1932.

Track and Field

High excitement is created by this one area of sports and a great deal of attention is paid to it. All participating nations have shown great interest in these Olympic events. Track and Field competitions are said to be a true test of humans' basic athletic abilities—running, jumping, and throwing.

The first female athlete ever to enter the Olympics earned worldwide fame for her achievements in track and field. In the 1932 California Games, Mildred "Babe" Didrikson set world records in two events: the javelin throw and the 80-meter hurdles. Babe admitted that although she was born with some natural ability, her success came from her hard work in training and her strong desire to be the best.

Another American who earned the title of "Top Male Athlete" was Rafer Johnson. In 1960, his decathlon score (8683) topped all previous world records.

Of great interest to Olympic fans and athletes is the Marathon. However, the world's fastest marathon time was not achieved in Olympic competition. Derek Clayton of Australia ran the twenty-six

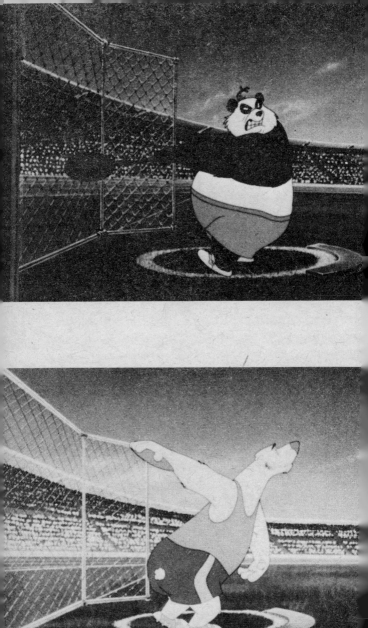

mile race in two hours, eight minutes and approximately thirty-three seconds (2:08:33.6). Well known American Olympic runner, Frank Shorter won a gold medal in 1972 for his time of 2:12:19.8.

Who is the world's fastest human? Who can jump the highest? Who has the most endurance? These questions are all decided by the Olympic track and field competitions.

There are thirty-seven events: twenty-three for men and fourteen for women. These include: Running—100-meter, 200-meter, 400-meter, 800-meter, 1500-meter, 5000-meter and 10,000-meter distances. Also included is the twenty-six mile Marathon run. Scoring in these track events is done by an electronic device and a photo-finish camera; Hurdles—running a set course that includes high and low hurdles. Completion time as well as skill in jumping hurdles determines the winner; Relays—four athletes on each team run an equal distance and pass a "baton" to the next runner on the team; Jumps—broad jump (a leap for distance), high jump (a jump over a high bar), pole vault (a high jump with the aid of a pole), and triple jump (a combination of a hop, a step, and a broad jump). The winner jumps the farthest (broad jump, triple jump) or the highest (high jump, pole vault); Throws—shot put (a metal ball weighing 16 pounds for men and 8 pounds 13 ounces for women); discus (a saucerlike object weighing 5 pounds, 6.55 ounces for men and 2 pounds 3.27 ounces for women); javelin (a spear weighing 28.22 ounces and measuring 102 1/3 to 106 1/3 centimeters for men and 21.16 ounces, 86 2/3 to 90 ½ centimeters for women); hammer (a metal ball on a chain), an event for men only. The distance of each throw determines the winners.

Separate Olympic medals are awarded to the high scorer in each event.

Shooting

Shooting as a sport was made popular long ago by hunters and gun exhibitionists. Rifle and Pistol Shooting was included in the first modern Olympics (1896).

It is probably one of the most difficult Olympic events to follow. Shooting competitions vary in distances, positions, targets, and guns. There are so many different types of skills that can be tested. Contests include: small-bore rifle (three positions), small-bore rifle prone position, rapid-fire pistol, trap shooting, skeet shooting, and running game target.

Women shooters are allowed to enter the same competitions as men.

Basketball

Basketball is the only Olympic sport that originated in America. And today, more people in the United States watch basketball than any other sport.

Olympic basketball is played indoors on a hardwood floor. There are five players on each team, and they have the positions of guard (two), forward (two), or center (one). Points are scored by shooting the ball into the opposite team's basket. Players not only try to score, but also try to prevent the other team from scoring.

Olympic basketball teams have been noted for their talented players. Many young men become stars in professional basketball.

Women's teams were included in this Olympic event beginning in 1976. In only a short time the United States has produced several high-scoring women players.

Canoeing

The sport of Canoeing is said to have been created by the Olympics. Its popularity has spread all over the world.

There are two types of canoeing contests in the Olympics—Kayaks and Canadian. In kayaks, the paddle used has a blade at both ends. In Canadian, the paddle has only one blade which must be moved from one side of the canoe to the other.

The events for men are: kayak singles, doubles, and fours, and Canadian singles and doubles. The women compete only in kayak singles and doubles. Races are conducted to determine semifinalists and finalists in each contest.

Equestrian Sports

Equestrian means riding on horseback. These competitions are the only Olympic events in which animals are used.

Women compete on the same teams as men. In 1952, Marjorie B. Haines was the first woman member of a U.S. equestrian team.

There are three events in this competition: Dressage—moving the horse through a set course to demonstrate the degree of understanding between the horse and the rider. Points from 10 (excellent) to 0 are awarded for each movement; Grand Prix Jumping—riding a course consisting of twelve to fifteen jumps of different heights and widths. Riders receive faults for knocking down an obstacle or for not jumping it; Three Day Event—completing a series of tests to show riding ability. There are three tests performed by the same rider on the same horse. The first day is the Dressage; the second, the Endurance Test; and the third, the Show-Jumping. Teams and individuals win by scoring the least penalties or the most points.

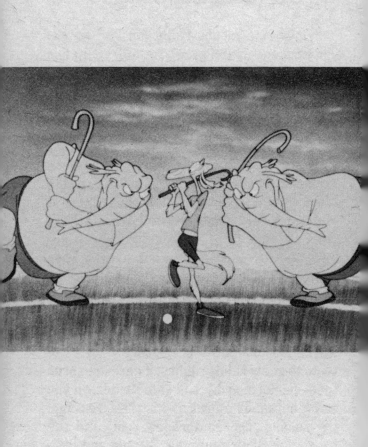

Field Hockey

The game of Field Hockey is considered the forerunner of baseball. The first of the stick-and-ball games, field hockey became an Olympic team sport in 1908.

The field hockey team consists of eleven players and two substitutes—five forwards, three halfbacks, two fullbacks, and a goal keeper. Each game is started by a "bully," similar to a jump ball in basketball. A bully also begins the play after a goal is scored. Two opposing players face each other in the center of the field and try to take control of the ball for their team. The object of the game is to score a goal by hitting the ball into the opponents' net.

Since field hockey is a widely popular sport among women, their teams also compete in this event.

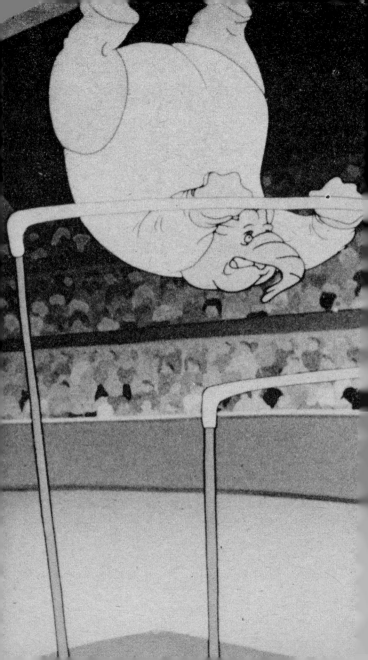

Gymnastics

Until recently, Gymnastics was one of the least popular Olympic sports. The 1976 Games at Montreal produced a star who has gained fame for her gymnastic performance. Fourteen-year-old Nadia Comaneci of Romania received a perfect score of 10 on the opening day of competition.

Gymnastics is said to be one of the most graceful and beautiful sports to watch. Yet those who participate show courage, conditioning, and strength of their bodies.

Men and women participate in both team and individual competitions. Each contestant must perform one required exercise and one of his or her own choosing. Team scores are based on the average of all their members' scores.

The major men's events are: horizontal bar, parallel bar, side horse, rings, horse vault, and floor exercises. Women compete on uneven bars, balance beam, horse vault, and floor exercises.

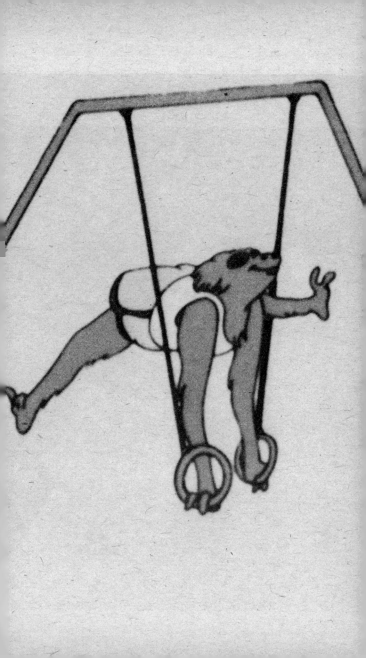

Fencing

Fencing became a sport after it was no longer a method of self-defense. Today it is an exciting Olympic sport for both men and women competitors.

There are three types of fencing for men, each using different weapons—foil, épée, and saber. Women use only one weapon—foil.

The three weapons differ in their points, blade edge and handguard shape.

Each weapon aims for different body targets. To win, a fencer must score five hits (for men) or four hits (for women) in a given time. The period of play is called a "bout," and is six minutes for men and five minutes for women.

Competitors in all types of fencing contests wear masks, gloves, and protective clothing.

Rowing

Seven events are included in the Olympic rowing sports. These are: single sculls, double sculls, pair oars with coxswains, pair oars without coxswains, four oars with coxswains, four oars without coxswains, and the eight-oared shell.

Sculling is rowing with two oars, one in each hand. Rowing is propelling the boat with only one oar, that oar being held in both hands. The coxswain is the person who steers the boat but does not row. The size of the boat varies with the number of members in the crew. For example, in pair oars without coxswain, the most difficult of the contests, the boat is 32 feet long and weighs about 65 pounds. Two crew members race this boat.

The Olympic race course for rowing is 2000 meters, or about 1¼ miles long.

America has continually been successful in the eight-oared shell competition because this type of rowing is a popular collegiate sport.

Boxing

Boxing is one of the oldest sports. In the ancient Olympic Games, boxers wore straps of leather around their fists and arms. There were no rounds or regular rest periods. Contests lasted until one man was knocked out or surrendered.

Today, Olympic boxers wear special padded headgear to protect them from serious injury. Modern boxing gloves are also padded, unlike the hard ones of the ancient Olympic competitors. Boxers are put into weight classes in order to insure a fair fight.

Although boxing is a dangerous sport, it fits well into the Olympic theme. The tradition of fair play and sportsmanship is carried out in every match.

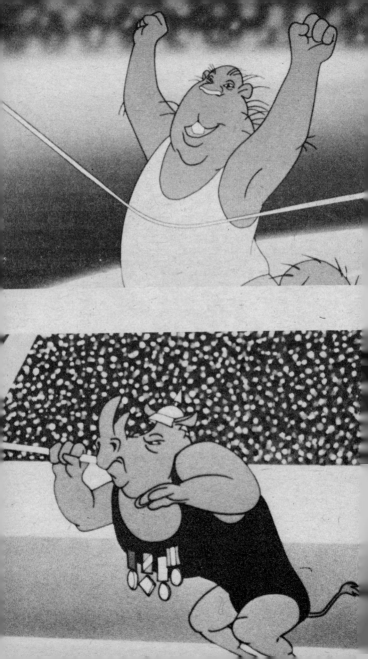

Modern Pentathlon

The most important of all the skills needed in this great contest is endurance. It is said that the winner of the modern Pentathlon displays all around athletic excellence.

This contest requires each athlete to participate in five events: running broad jump, javelin throw, 200-meter race, discus throw, and 1500-meter flat race.

Jim Thorpe, a United States Indian, gained worldwide fame as "The World's Greatest Athlete" for winning this competition in 1912.

Yachting

Yachting is the Olympic sport of racing small boats. There are six classes of competition determined by the size and type of the boat: Soling, Finn, Flying Dutchman, 470 Class, Tornado, and Tempest.

Seven races are run in each class, of which the best six count in the score. For each race, points are awarded to contestants by the order in which they finish. At the end of the races, the points are totaled to determine the winner.

For the yachting event, women do not have their own races. They are invited to compete alongside the men.

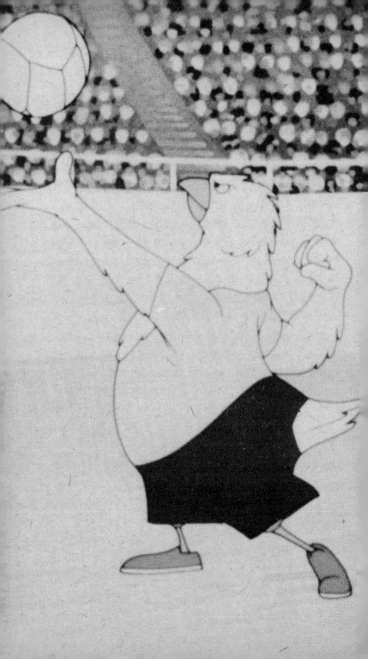

Volleyball

Volleyball is an indoor team sport. It is a ball game played on a court 30 by 60 feet. The net in the center of the court is 8 feet high for men, and 7 feet 4¼ inches high for women. There are six players on each team.

The ball is put into play with a serve. Only the serving team can win points. If the ball is missed by the serving team, the opposing team then serves.

Volleyball teams must compete in qualifying competitions before they can enter the Olympic Games.

Team Handball

Team Handball is a game that resembles American football. In Olympic competition the sport is played indoors by teams of twelve players.

The game is played with a small, round, rubber ball. The object is to score points by getting the ball over the goal line, between the posts and under the cross bar. Players move around the court bouncing the ball or passing it. The ball may be touched by all parts of the body *except* the feet.

The men's game is played in two thirty-minute periods; the women's in two twenty-five minute periods. Both have a ten-minute rest between periods.

Judo

Judo first became an Olympic sport in 1964 during the games held in Tokyo. Originally an ancient method of self-defense, judo became a sport nearly 100 years ago.

The skill of judo is based on a combination of strength and balance. The contests are fought on a mat under the control of a referee. Points are awarded to the participant showing good judo technique. Violations are scored against players for poor performance. Competition is in six weight divisions. The winners of all the classes meet to decide an overall champion.

Cycling

Bicycling has gained worldwide popularity as a sport, as well as a means of transportation. Olympic competition is in two categories—track events and road events.

Track events include: 1000-meter sprint; 4000-meter individual pursuit; 4000-meter team pursuit. There are usually four members on a team. The Road event is a 62.13 mile (100 kilometer) team road race.

Archery

Men and women have their own contests in archery. However, the rules are the same for both in these competitions of skill with a bow and arrow.

The target is 4 feet in diameter. It is divided into five rings, each of a different color. The rings are further divided into "inner" and "outer" rings. The highest score for a shot is ten points earned for a bull's eye, an arrow in the inner gold ring. The lowest score is one point for an arrow in the outer white ring.

The round is the official period of play. Each player takes 144 shots and can score a maximum of 1440 points.

Soccer

The game of soccer is a form of ancient football. Prior to the year 1900, it was popular strictly among European countries. However, when Olympic competition drew worldwide attention to the sport, soccer became the most popular team game in the world.

Unlike American football, the game of soccer is very simple. Only seventeen rules guide the game. Eleven players, including the goalie, comprise each team. The object of the game is to score the most points by passing the ball between the posts and into the goal.

America has never won a gold medal in this event. Latin American and European teams have dominated the sport.

Weightlifting

Among the most exciting Olympic events is this modern test of strength. Weightlifters compete in nine bodyweight classes similar to those of boxing and wrestling. In each class contestants participate in two exercises: the snatch, and the clean and jerk. For each lift the contestant must hold the weight for the referee's count of "one, two." The scores in the two exercises are totaled to determine the final score.

If two weightlifters tie by lifting the same total weight, the person with the lower body weight is declared the winner.